The MIDDLE AGES

Revised and Updated

JANE SHUTER

Heinemann Library
Chicago, Illinois

Customer Service 888-454-2279
Visit our website at www.heinemannraintree.com

Designed by Richard Parker and Q2A Solutions
Printed in China by WKT Ltd

11 10 09 08 07
10 9 8 7 6 5 4 3 2 1

New edition ISBNs: 1-403-48813-4 (hardcover)
                   1-403-48820-7 (paperback)

13 digit ISBNs: 978-1-403-48813-8 (hardcover)
                978-1-403-48820-6 (paperback)

The Library of Congress has cataloged the first edition as follows:
Shuter, Jane.
    The Middle Ages / Jane Shuter.
    p.   cm. — (History opens windows)
    Includes bibliographical references and index.
    Summary: An introduction to the various elements of life in the Middle Ages, including religion, knights, castles, family life, and food.
    ISBN 1-57572-886-9 (lib. bdg.)
    1. Middle Ages—History—Juvenile literature. 2. Civilization, Medieval—Juvenile literature.
    [1. Middle Ages. 2. Civilization, Medieval.]   I. Title. II. Series.
    Dl17.S53   1999
    956—dc21
                              99-11818
                                CIP
                                AC

Acknowledgments
The publisher would like to thank the following for permission to reproduce photographs: The Royal Collection, Her Majesty Queen Elizabeth II, p. **6**; Masters & Fellows of Corpus Christi College, Cambs, p. **8**; British Library, pp. **11**, **13**, **14**, **18**; Bridgeman Art Library/Louvre, Paris, p. **16**; Salisbury Museum, p. **19**; Bridgeman Art Library, p. **20**; Bridgeman Art Library/Castello del Buonconsiglio, p. **21**; Varberg, p. **23**; Bridgeman Art Library/British Library, pp. **24**, **25**; Bibliotheque Royale Albert I, Bruxelles, p. **27**; Giraudon/Bibl. De l'Arsenal, p. **29**; Wellcome Institute Library, London, p. **30**.
Illustrations: Eileen Mueller Neill, pp. **4**, **10**; John James, p. **6**; Bill Le Fever, pp. **9**, **15**, **17**; Michael Holford, p.**12**; Richard Hook, pp. **22-23**; James Fields, p. **26**; Finbarr O'Connor, p. **28**.

Cover photograph reproduced with permission of Ancience Art & Architecture Collection Ltd / Prisma.

Contents

Some words are shown in bold, **like this**.
You can find out what they mean by looking in the glossary.

Introduction

This is a map of Europe in about 1100. European countries were led by powerful ruling families and their borders were always changing.

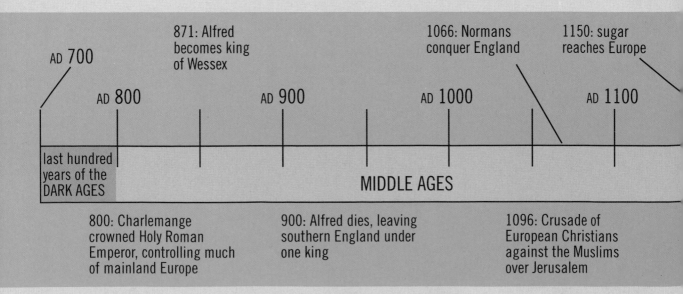

The Middle Ages did not happen just in one country, nor did this time in history have a definite beginning or end. It happened all over Europe between about 800 and 1450, but it began and ended at different times in different places.

The Middle Ages followed the Dark Ages, a time when there was little knowledge or progress. The name Dark Ages describes when the Romans no longer ruled and Europe was settled by small **tribes** with different leaders.

During the Middle Ages, countries became more settled and developed new ways of ruling. The Catholic Church was the religion of almost everyone in Europe. People became more interested in learning and in exploration. The Middle Ages was the bridge between the Dark Ages and the next period of development, called the Renaissance.

1215: Magna Carta in England forces the king to share power

1346–53: the Black Death

1454: First book printed on a printing press

1492: Columbus reaches the Americas

AD 1200   AD 1300   AD 1400   AD 1500   AD 1600

MIDDLE AGES

1275: Marco Polo reaches the court of Kubla Kahn

1337: 1453 the Hundred Years War

first hundred years of the RENAISSANCE

Rulers in the Middle Ages

Alfred ruled Wessex, in south England. In 878, the Vikings drove him out. However, Alfred beat them back and then took over other tribes until he ruled all of England.

The first rulers in the Middle Ages were the leaders of various **tribes** in each country. They had to be good war leaders because each group was constantly trying to take over more land. Land belonged to the tribe, and all the men fought to defend it and capture more.

The ruler was the most important person in the tribe, but the ruler could be replaced. When the ruler died, a member of his family could become the ruler, or the tribe could choose a new leader.

As the Middle Ages went on, European rulers gained more land and power. Rulers began to see the land as their own, rather than shared with all the people. They gave land to others in return for loyalty. Giving land in return for loyalty is called a **feudal system**. Those with the most land were the most important. They could give land to less important people. Land was given in turn down to the least important **peasants**, who farmed the land for their **lord**.

When he died, a ruler passed his kingdom to his sons. If the sons were babies and could not rule, then someone else ruled until they were old enough to take over. When a ruler had no sons, his male relatives often quarreled over who would be king.

European rulers had different groups of people to advise them. In England, at the beginning of the Middle Ages, Alfred had advisors but ruled alone. By the end of the Middle Ages, kings had to listen to elected **parliaments**. This picture from 1295 shows Edward I and his parliament.

Religion

During the Middle Ages, most of the people in Europe became Christians. Countries had an **official religion**. Churches and cathedrals were built everywhere. At this time there was only one kind of Christian worship. All Christians were Catholics. They obeyed the **Pope**, who is the leader of the Catholic Church.

Catholicism gave European kingdoms a feeling of unity. They were especially united against threats from people outside of Europe who had different religious beliefs. The church had a system based on importance, just like the government. Often, the most important church leaders also played an important part in ruling the country. Many church leaders were more interested in money and power than in religion.

As the **nobles** watch, this ruler is being crowned by the most powerful churchmen in his country.

Not all religious people were involved in government. Monks were men who shut themselves away from the world. They lived in monasteries to pray and serve God. Women who did this were called nuns, and they lived in convents.

Monasteries had enough land for the monks to grow their own food and to grow herbs for medicines.

The leader of each monastery was called an abbot. He had his own set of rooms.

Monks tried to live very simply. They slept in large rooms called dormitories.

Monks spent much of the time praying.

Monks ate their meals together, while one read aloud from the *Bible*.

Trade and Exploration

This was the known world of the Middle Ages. A few explorers, such as Marco Polo, had traveled further. People knew China and India existed, but they did not know their size and shape. They had no idea that Australia or the Americas even existed.

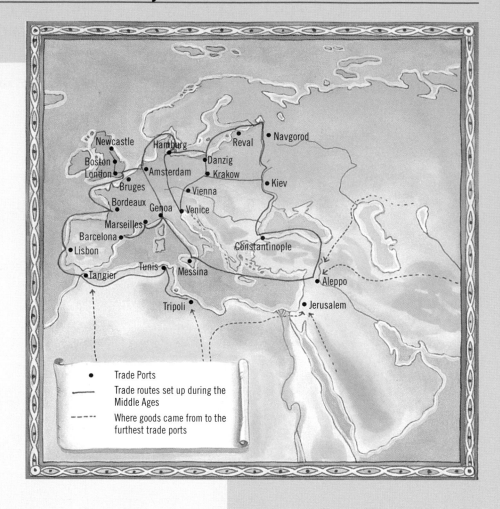

Newcastle
Boston
London
Bruges
Bordeaux
Marseilles
Barcelona
Lisbon
Tangier
Hamburg
Amsterdam
Genoa
Vienna
Venice
Tunis
Messina
Tripoli
Reval
Danzig
Krakow
Constantinople
Navgorod
Kiev
Aleppo
Jerusalem

- Trade Ports
— Trade routes set up during the Middle Ages
--- Where goods came from to the furthest trade ports

During the Middle Ages, people began to think about exploring new lands. **Goods** from these other lands, such as silk from China and spices from India, were beginning to reach Europe. The nobility of Europe wanted to show their power. Power was closely linked to wealth, and one way to show your wealth was to buy expensive fabrics and foods from foreign lands.

Wealthy people did not travel to get these luxury goods. Instead, **merchants** made the dangerous journeys. If they traveled overland, there was danger from robbers and difficult travel on muddy, unpaved roads. If they traveled by sea, their ships might be lost in storms.

So why did they go to all this trouble? They did it for money. They could buy spices, silks, and other luxury goods cheaply in the far away countries and then sell them at a profit in Europe. Traders could pay all the costs of their journey and still have a lot of money left.

Sea travel was often easier than overland travel, even though the single-sailed boats were small. There were few navigational aids or accurate maps to help traders travel to far away lands.

Knights

The **feudal system** meant that **lords** and other important people had to fight for their rulers. They also had to provide knights to fight. Knights were given land by their lords. They were expected to fight when the lords told them to.

Knights wore heavy protective metal clothes called armor. They fought with long spears called lances when they were on horseback. If they came off their horses, they fought with swords. It took a great deal of training to fight well in armor. Knights were trained in **noble** families by other knights. Knights showed off their skills at competitions called tournaments.

A knight in full armor leads his men to war.

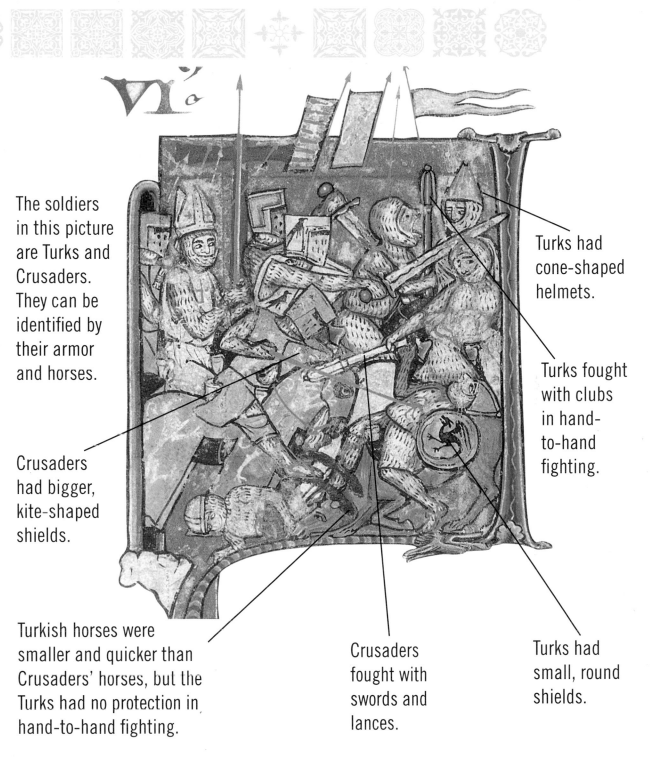

The soldiers in this picture are Turks and Crusaders. They can be identified by their armor and horses.

Crusaders had bigger, kite-shaped shields.

Turkish horses were smaller and quicker than Crusaders' horses, but the Turks had no protection in hand-to-hand fighting.

Crusaders fought with swords and lances.

Turks had cone-shaped helmets.

Turks fought with clubs in hand-to-hand fighting.

Turks had small, round shields.

Armies from all over Europe united several times to fight a common religious enemy, the Turks. They fought because the **Pope** told them to take the city of Jerusalem from the Turks, who were Muslims. Jerusalem is in modern-day Israel. It is important to Jews, Muslims, and Christians.

Castles

The first castles of the Middle Ages were wooden forts on top of a steep mound. They were built to keep soldiers safe in enemy territory. They had wooden walls all the way around and a defensive tower inside. The tower was taller than the walls.

Wooden castles were easy to build, but they were cramped and uncomfortable. They were ideal as quick, temporary protection. But wooden walls can be battered down or set on fire more easily than stone walls. From 1100 onwards, more permanent stone castles were built. Stone castles became the homes of wealthy **lords**. The lords used castles to show their power, and they wanted comfort, not just defense.

This tapestry picture shows French soldiers building an early wooden castle in about 1060.

A Stone Castle

Stone castles had private rooms for the lords and their families.

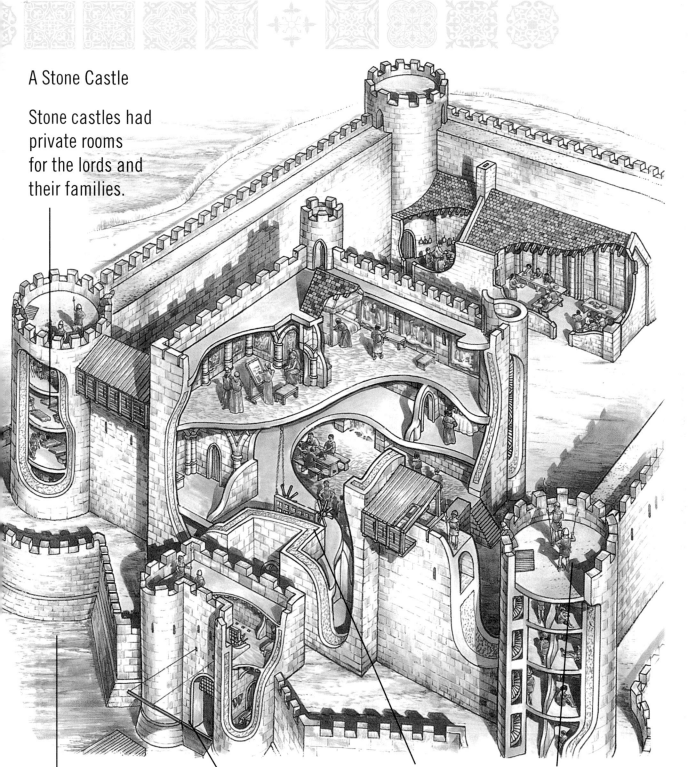

The deep ditch around this castle has been filled with water to make a moat.

The drawbridge could be raised if the castle was attacked.

The iron, grid-like portcullis just behind the drawbridge could be lowered to the ground to form another barrier.

Soldiers could throw things down onto attackers from the top of the walls.

Town Life

Large towns and cities in the Middle Ages were often centers of trade. The wealthy **merchants** and **craftworkers** lived in these towns and cities. People came from miles around to shop, to see the religious **mystery plays**, or to go to the large **fairs**. Poorer people lived there, too. They worked for wealthy craftworkers or ran their own small shops or inns. Several very poor families might live in a single room, but they were luckier than the beggars who slept on the street.

A small town might be the trading center for the villages around it. Farm produce and animals would be bought and sold on market days. A few craftworkers in the town might make shoes or pots for sale. There might even be an annual fair with acrobats, jugglers, and other entertainment.

The best craftworkers often lived in the biggest towns. This sacrament cup was made in Limoges, France. Craftworkers there were famous for mixing enamels with gold and jewels.

Houses in a Medieval Town

Even the homes of wealthy people had less furniture and possessions in them than modern homes.

The houses in this town have slate roofs. If slate was not available locally, then thatch or terra-cotta tiles were used.

Buildings in towns were often made from a wooden framework filled by wattle and daub. Wattle and daub is woven sticks filled with clay or mud. The walls are then plastered.

This is the home of a successful shoemaker. The store is on the ground floor facing the street. The workshop is behind the store.

Craftworkers in the Middle Ages could not work unless they joined a **guild**. They had to pay to join and prove that they could make **goods** to a high standard. This meeting in a guild hall could be to accept a new member or to punish someone for trading without being a member.

Country Life

In the Middle Ages, the European countryside was scattered with patches of land held by various **lords**. This land included all the villages and farms.

The people who lived there were mostly **peasants**. Their homes belonged to the lord, and they worked for him. They could not move away without his permission, but he could throw them out of their homes at any time. If a peasant worker was injured and could not work, he and his family might be homeless. The lord might want the cottage as a home for a new worker.

A peasant guides the plow that turns over the soil. The peasant behind him sows the seeds. The peasant in front guides the oxen.

Most peasants stayed in one place all their lives. They worked the land and brought up their children to work on the land after them. They farmed the lord's land for part of each year. The rest of the time, they farmed the land the lord allowed them to use. For this, they gave the lord a share of their crops. Their land was often made up of several long, thin strips in huge fields that the villagers shared. This meant that everyone got a share of both the good and the bad land.

The lord's **court** decided how many strips each peasant got and where the strips were in the field. The court also settled disputes between villagers and handed out punishment for local crimes.

These are shears from the Middle Ages. They were used to cut the wool from sheep each year.

Families

In the Middle Ages, people did not live as long as they do today. If they survived the diseases of early childhood, and did not die in battle, they might live to the age of 50. Women sometimes died in childbirth. Because of this, people often married more than once.

Children were important to families, especially boys. They were expected to take over their family's land or business. Couples usually had several children very quickly after they married. Some of the children would die. Wealthy families sent their teenage children to another family, where they were taught the skills they would need in adult life.

Children of **peasants** began working with their parents as soon as they were strong enough to do farm work.

Wealthy families chose who their children married. They often arranged marriages when children were very small to form links between families.

Clothes

In the Middle Ages, clothes were very important. They showed a person's wealth and importance in two ways. First, wealthy people wore long robes with long, flowing sleeves. They wore shoes with very long, pointed ends. These clothes would have been impossible to wear while working, so they showed that the people who wore them did not need to work.

Expensive fabrics, such as brightly colored silks and velvets trimmed with jewels and fur, also told the importance of the person wearing them. Many European countries had laws about who could wear certain colors, fabrics, and furs. These rules were often changed and updated.

A **lord**, his lady, and his servants wore bright colors. Ordinary people wore plain clothes that were easy to work in and were cheaper to make.

Here are a hood and leggings from about 1360. They were found in a bog in Sweden. Very few other medieval clothes have survived.

Food

The illustrations on these pages are from a book made for Sir Geoffrey Luttrell in about 1330. They show the cooks preparing rabbits and chickens as the family eats from silver dishes.

What people ate in the Middle Ages depended on their wealth. Wealthy people ate fine, white bread. They ate a variety of meat, including pork, beef, lamb, chicken, duck, and goose. They also hunted and ate wild animals, such as deer. On special days in the religious year, they had to eat fish. They ate fruit and vegetables and usually drank wine. Their food was flavored with sugar and spices.

Less wealthy people did not eat as well as this. They ate more ordinary and less expensive meat, fish, fruit, vegetables, and wine. Their food was prepared more simply. They used honey instead of sugar, and they used less spice to flavor their food.

Poor people seldom ate meat. Sometimes they might have a piece of bacon. They ate vegetables, cheese, and bread made from coarse, dark flour. **Peasants** ate their chickens that no longer laid eggs. They hunted and ate wild animals, such as rabbits. They grew their own vegetables and sometimes raised a pig or two for meat.

The very poor had to beg for food. Christians were told that God wanted them to care for the poor, so they often gave beggars leftover food. At wealthy homes, servants might give beggars the bread plates that the people had used to hold their meal. A bread plate looked like a flat pizza.

Plague!

In 1346, a **plague** from Asia swept into Europe. In Asia, most people were **immune** to the plague or only became mildly ill. Europeans were not immune. The highly contagious plague flowed westward, moving most quickly along trade routes. At first it was like a cold. Then swellings appeared in the groin and armpits. Black patches then broke out all over the body, giving the plague its name of the Black Death.

We now know that the plague was spread by the bites of fleas that lived on rats. This explains why it was often worse in crowded cities where rats could live in the garbage thrown onto the streets. But in the Middle Ages, no one knew what caused the plague or how to cure it.

These people are flagellants. They believed that the plague was God's punishment for people's sins. They traveled all over Europe whipping themselves and praying for the forgiveness of everyone.

Plague victims are buried at Tournai in the modern Netherlands.

How many people died of the plague? In some places almost no one became ill. In other places almost everyone died. It is hard to know how many died, but historians think it was about one out of every three people.

The plague caused huge problems in everyday life. At first, the dead were buried individually in coffins with a proper religious service. But soon there were so many dead that they were buried in the sheets they died in, in huge pits in the ground, and sometimes without a religious service. This upset families because they believed that without a proper burial, the dead people would not go to heaven.

A Changed Europe

Before the **plague**, the **feudal system** worked because there were plenty of **peasants** to work the land. The plague changed all that. Some **lords** had trouble finding enough workers, especially at busy times, such as the harvest. The surviving peasants began to ask for better working conditions or their freedom.

If the peasants did not get what they wanted, they left. In some places, peasants turned to violence to get what they wanted.

In the early Middle Ages, the lord was in control, but the Black Death changed this.

The plague affected everyone. Workers in towns also demanded better conditions. Survivors had less competition for work and profits, so they made more money. Less food was produced and fewer **goods** were made. This caused prices to rise, but not too much, because there were fewer people and less of a need for food and goods.

The plague shook people emotionally. Many people came to see that change was possible. They saw that they could try to make a good life for themselves and did not have to accept the life to which they were born. A French writer in 1359 wrote that after the plague, people were more mean and greedy, even though they were better off than before. This was not true of everyone, but a change in thinking was an important result of the plague.

This French picture from about 1400 shows French peasants asking their lord for their freedom.

A New Time

The new ways of thinking affected governments and the church as well. People began to think of themselves less as Europeans united by religion and more as separate countries. Rulers began to question the right of the **Pope** to tell their people what to do. People began to have new ideas about religion, government, medicine, art, and almost everything else. These ideas spread and the Middle Ages moved, at different times in different places, to a new age—the Renaissance.

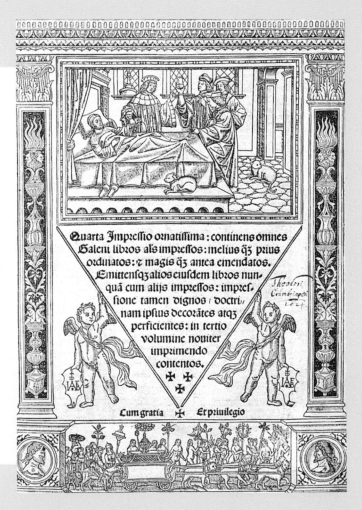

With the invention of the printing press, books became more widely available and could be used to spread new ideas. This is a page from a medical book, first printed in about 1460.

Glossary

court   place where a group of people decide if someone has broken the law and what punishment should be given

craftworker   person who makes things for a living

fair   regular gathering in a place where people come to buy and sell and entertain

feudal system   system of governing a country in which the ruler gives a few important people land in return for obedience and loyalty

goods   things made or grown to sell

guild   group of people who work in the same trade

immune   not affected by an illness

lord   important person

merchant   person who buys things from one person and sells them to others

mystery play   play that tells a story from the *Bible*

noble   important person

official religion   religion the government says people must follow

parliament   group of government officials that makes a country's laws

peasant   poor farmworker

plague   widespread and deadly disease

Pope   leader of the Catholic Church, who Christians in all countries during the Middle Ages had to obey, even before obeying their ruler

tribe   group of people with the same leader

Find Out More

Books to read
History of Britain: Medieval Britain 1066–1485, Brenda Williams (Heinemann Library, 2006)
Art in History: Art of the Middle Ages, Jennifer Olmsted (Heinemann Library, 2006)

Using the Internet
Explore the Internet to find out more about the Middle Ages. Use a search engine, such as www.yahooligans.com or www.internet4kids.com and type in a keyword or phrase such as "medieval castles" or "plague".

Index